"light? it's a difficult one, that." **Elliot**

"there's light everywhere! big swirls everywhere! i'm gonna do it in different colours, this yellow is good, i can only see it when the torch shines on it" **Emily**

Protagonists

Aidan 3 years, 5 months
Amber 3 years, 0 months
Amerie 3 years, 2 months
Arden 4 years, 1 month
Ashlei 3 years, 10 months
Axel 3 years, 3 months
Caitlin 3 years, 3 months
Charlie B. 4 years, 1 month
Charlie P. 3 years, 2 months
Cordelia 3 years, 8 months
Ela 3 years, 3 months
Elliot 3 years, 1 month
Emilia 3 years, 0 months
Emily 3 years, 10 months
Erin 3 years, 2 months
Evie 3 years, 2 months
Ewa 3 years, 11 months
Frankie 3 years, 3 months
Gabrielle A. 4 years, 0 months
Gabrielle P. 3 years, 3 months
Harry 3 years, 7 months
Hughie 2 years, 8 months
Iggy 3 years, 3 months
Imogen 3 years, 4 months

James 3 years, 0 months
Jasper 3 years, 6 months
Josh 2 years, 10 months
Juliusz 4 years, 2 months
Katie 3 years, 7 months
Keira 3 years, 11 months
Kyran 3 years, 1 month
Lachlan 3 years, 8 months
Leo 3 years, 5 months
Lewis 3 years, 10 months
Macey 3 years, 0 months
Madison 3 years, 8 months
Molly 3 years, 3 months
Mya 2 years, 10 months
Natalie 2 years, 10 months
Noa 3 years, 10 months
Olivia 2 years, 11 months
Ruby 3 years, 1 month
Saffy 3 years, 11 months
Scarlett 3 years, 7 months
Stanley 3 years, 3 months
Sukie 3 years, 1 month
Tadiwa 2 years, 7 months
Thomas 3 years, 7 months
Zach 3 years, 9 months
Zachary 3 years, 8 months
Zara 3 years, 11 months

Acknowledg[...]ty of children, parents and staff at Reflections Nursery

FOREWORD

At Reflections Nursery in Worthing, UK we draw much inspiration from the world-renowned infant-toddler centres and pre-schools of Reggio Emilia in Northern Italy. Work with pre-school children in Reggio Emilia does not follow a prescribed 'curriculum'. Teachers support children to investigate their theories leading to long-term projects or 'progettazione'. As Carlina Rinaldi, one of the leading pedagogues in Reggio describes, they follow a 'contextual curriculum', based on, "…a strategy, a daily practice of observation-interpretation-documentation." [1]

At Reflections we seek to work in a similar way with children, always paying significant attention to children working as a group. There is recognition in Reggio that when children work together their divergent theories and opinions are considered a resource:

> *"For children to be in a group is a situation of great privilege, as if inside a great, transforming laboratory."*
>
> Loris Malaguzzi

Educators at Reflections document children's daily experiences using photos, notes, films and sound recordings. We find such documentation helps facilitate reflection on the learning processes of both children and adults and contributes to educators' own professional development.

It is worth noting that documenting children's learning has, over time, deeply influenced the culture at Reflections and become a reference point for dialogue between educators and parents, and the wider community.

Many of the projects in Reflections Nursery begin with a 'provocation' - an object or an idea presented to children as a group for their opinion, theory or investigation. Often a provocation will come from the children themselves or may be present in the nursery environment. For example, we brought in a taxidermy crocodile head which prompted a project entitled Crocodiles!, subsequently documented in the first book from On Reflection Publishing.

Reflections Nursery has seen the value an artist can bring to working with groups of young children, especially in supporting them to develop their many 'languages' of expression.

----

(1) In Dialogue with Reggio Emilia, Carlina Rinaldi 2006.

Angela Chick joined the nursery in July 2009 with little experience of working with children but with a background as an artist and much enthusiasm, intelligence and resourcefulness. In two years, Angela has become a reflective educator and a valued member of the pedagogical team at the nursery; her passion for documenting children's learning has led her to write this second project workbook.

Light Everywhere! presents a series of snapshots from one of many projects which children follow at Reflections. It captures selected moments from a period of six months when a large group of children were deeply engaged with investigating light, and the properties and effects of light. We hope to give visibility to children's potential by documenting this project but acknowledge that we will surely have missed opportunities for children to experience and express their potential during the course of the project and we welcome all feedback in this regard.

> *"Documentation... is seen as a way of listening to, respecting and supporting individuals in their search to find meaning in the world."*
> Carlina Rinaldi

At Reflections our aim is to support early years educators to develop their own understanding of how children learn. In Light Everywhere! we have chosen to present children's experiences; leaving space for other educators to construct their own interpretation of the children's learning. As in our previous publication, Crocodile!, we have omitted any significant analysis, neither have we sought to link children's learning with curriculum guidelines.

In documenting project work there are always choices to be made in deciding what to include or omit – Angela took over 1400 photos in the course of this project, along with notes and videos - we recognise that this book is a highly subjective presentation.

At Reflections we believe that documentation is an important instrument in children's own learning - enabling children to see themselves in a new light, and revisit and re-interpret experiences in which they were the protagonists. All the children involved in this project received a copy of this book.

In every educational establishment choices are made about values and ethics. Reflections Nursery chooses to see itself as a community and a place of creating connections, interactions and dialogue amongst its citizens, younger and older, and the citizens of the wider community. It is our aim to establish shared values and influence a shared future, and it is in this spirit that we would like to share this book with you.

Martin Pace
Director, Reflections Nursery & Forest School, Worthing   September 2011

INTRODUCTION

In late 2010, children aged three and four years in the pre-school section of Reflections Nursery, Worthing had been involved in a project about crocodiles. Towards the end of this project the children were exploring light and shadow. They had created crocodile dens from luxurious fabrics and were using torchlight so their "crocodile eyes" could see. As they mapped the movement of crocodiles, they also began to map the beams of light.

They used an overhead projector with a taxidermy crocodile head to project giant crocodile shadows on the walls that would chase them around the Atelier (1) . I chose to introduce a variety of light provocations to support deeper exploration for the children.

A project began to emerge about investigating light and shadow, and children chose to access a variety of different light sources. They had the opportunity to test their theories about the characteristics of light – these included what colour light is, how it travels and how it works. Through their own investigations the children developed new understandings about light and its properties.

The Atelier became a laboratory filled with instruments for the investigation of light. We used a projector screen to play with our shadows from the overhead projector and to create beautiful shadow collages and light sculptures. A variety of torches were introduced which allowed the children to experiment with light 'travel', colour, transparency, and reflection.

Various colours of cellophane were displayed on interior windows allowing a soft flow of colour to stream through the Atelier. We used a blackout blind on the exterior windows to create a darkroom, allowing us to experiment with black light (or ultra violet light). Glowsticks were introduced as a provocation when the children insisted that light was white. There was a popular theory amongst the children that glowsticks were powered by batteries. It wasn't until some of their friends began to suggest that light emanated from "glow" inside that they began to reconsider their theory.

----

(1) The Atelier at Reflections Nursery is used as an art studio, a laboratory and a workshop; where theories can be explored and creative expression can be developed.

When black light was introduced this challenged a lot of the children's theories about light. How could light be 'black'? We explored the effect of black light on coloured objects and the children shared observations with their friends. The children dressed in fluorescent clothing and observed their glowing reflections in mirrors.

Interactive lights were introduced which gave children the power to control light with their voices and movement in a much more playful way than just flicking a switch. Children thought it was magic when they found they could turn a light on or off, or change the colour, by singing to it.

Alongside investigation and theorising there was also a lot of fun. The children used the space and resources in the Atelier to create their own light games and the room would fill with giggles as they saw their reflections in the black light.

"i see a shadow there! a shadow's coming!" Aidan

"i'm gonna make a shadow!"
Hughie

LIGHT + DARK

The children investigated shadow interaction from the initial stages of the project. Children were holding the crocodile head in front of the overhead projector running back and forth pretending a giant crocodile was going to get them. Some children initially did not like their own shadow but soon grew to be friends with it.

Arden's interactions with his shadow:
"i don't like my shadow! can't get me! shadows are always following you. but they never bang their heads. wait, where's my shadow gone?.. oh! he's there. i'm walking through it. when it's dark you can't see your shadow anymore. see? (he stands in front of my shadow) no shadow. but when it's light (he moves in front of the projector) it's always there. i'm playing with my shadow."
Arden

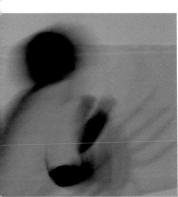

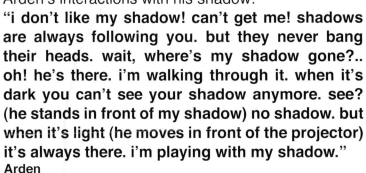

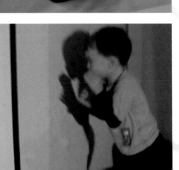

"shall we turn the shadows on?"
Caitlin asking to turn on the overhead projector

ARDEN COMPARING HANDS

Children would talk to their shadows and occasionally, when the overhead projector was turned off, some children believed that their shadows were hiding behind the projector screen and they would peek behind the screen to see if they could see them.

The children also observed how distance related to the sizes of their shadows. One day we were using the overhead projector and I put my hand onto it. As the image of my hand projected onto the screen Arden reached for my hand. He commented how his hand was smaller and suggested I put my hand on the screen and he would put his on the projector. I complied and he shared his observations:

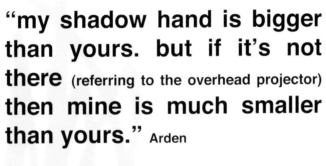

"my shadow hand is bigger than yours. but if it's not there (referring to the overhead projector) **then mine is much smaller than yours."** Arden

He removed his hand from the projector and held it up to mine to show me the difference.

Children began to talk about how they could change their shadows. Some wanted to try to create a larger shadow than their friends' while others wanted to make, "tiny little sneaky shadows."

"when you reach to the top of the ceiling that makes my shadow the biggest" **Aidan sharing discoveries about his shadow with his friends**

"i want pretty shells on it"
Ela

"LOTS of shells!"
Cordelia

SHADOW COMPOSITIONS
We experimented with shadow pictures using a variety of transparent papers and opaque objects. Cordelia, Ela and Emily chose to use the overhead projector to create a composition filled with seashells, which they projected onto the wall. They were very proud of their creation so we took a photograph of it for them.

They wanted to "make this picture to stay" so I decided to introduce light-reactive paper to them. When they created their compositions on the light-reactive paper, we exposed them to sunlight. As they rinsed the paper under water they were thrilled to see the image developing where it had been exposed to sunlight.

"we made them with different kinds of things. then we went outside quickly so no one saw us, and then we did some exercise and then we got them and we ran back inside and washed them and they turned colour" **Noa describing sun pictures, on light-reactive paper**

"it's magic!" **Macey**

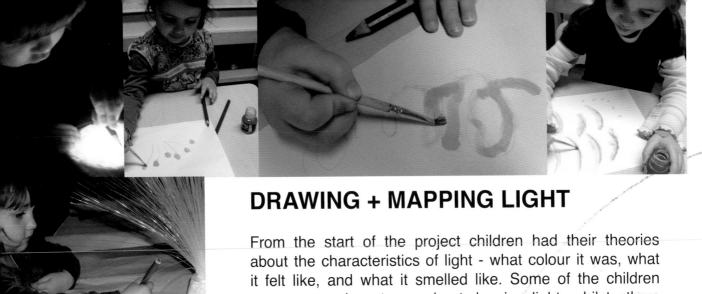

DRAWING + MAPPING LIGHT

From the start of the project children had their theories about the characteristics of light - what colour it was, what it felt like, and what it smelled like. Some of the children were unsure how to go about drawing light, whilst others came up with ingenious ideas. In their early explorations children would place a torch down on the table in front of them and trace the torchlight cascading across the table.

Jasper invented a variation by putting a piece of paper across the top of the torch and then tracing the light emerging. [See the *Layering Colour With Light* section]

"let's draw it! i want to draw it!" Zach

"we need water and a paintbrush and i need blue and yellow if i want to make green" Arden looking at a green glow stick

"can we draw when the light goes in and out?"
Stanley with light and mirrors

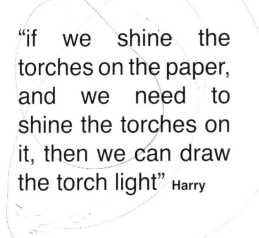

"if we shine the torches on the paper, and we need to shine the torches on it, then we can draw the torch light" Harry

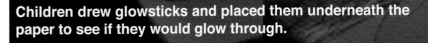

Children drew glowsticks and placed them underneath the paper to see if they would glow through.

"it's changing colours in the blur!"

Mya noticing colours blending

"these are my little circles of where the light things are" Emily

"it doesn't look like a rainbow, it looks like fireworks" **Zach**

There was also some interest in trying to draw with light. For this, we experimented with some slow shutter-speed photography. Children had a light of their choice and would move it as quickly as possible while I would take a photograph. We then reviewed the results together.

Around November 5th children chose to paint fireworks as there had been much fascination with Guy Fawkes Night.

"Butterflies" by Saffy & Zara

As more resources were made available the children used them in many different ways. When the glowsticks were introduced we started with only one or two different colours. The children chose to use these colours separately and it wasn't until a third colour was introduced that the children began using them together. Some children sorted them into colour groups and then made pictures using whatever colours they chose, putting them into linear patterns.

"i'm making a rainbow! our rainbow is gonna be the biggest rainbow! lots of colours. yellow, purple, orange and yellow. more and more colours" Ruby

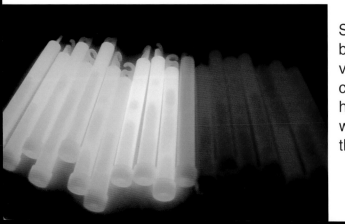

Saffy and Zara began making butterflies from glowsticks by laying them down on the table in an upturned v-shape and building with different colours. They created many variations. The children also constructed houses, letters, shapes, families, friends and castles with glowsticks. They were no longer just a light source, they became new construction and design materials.

"i'm gonna get all the yellows next to each other. trying to do all of these in a nice way. i'm concentrating really hard. these need to be standing straight. now reds, more candles. i'm gonna make a birthday cake"

Madison sharing her progress with her friends

"look! i made a triangle! i made an 'a'! i made a '4'! i made a 'L for Lachlan'; i made a square! i made a rectangle!" Lachlan moving the glowsticks around making different shapes

We created a dark room in the Atelier and lit it with black light. Keira and Imogen selected a number of glowsticks, and sat together at the table.

Keira said to Imogen "Let's make a line." "A long line" suggested Imogen. They built a line of glowsticks along the table by the black light. "That one goes there" said Imogen "And this one can go here" said Keira. "OK, I'll put my red one right there. I need to put this pinky red here. I'm making a line for you," said Imogen.

"i need to build a house"
Imogen

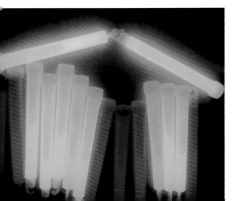

CHARLIE'S GLOWSTICK CASTLE

Charlie was working with the glowsticks: "We need to make a castle!" He carefully lined up only yellow glowsticks. Once he had a line of them, he moved on to orange and red. He spent the entire morning working on his castle with a friend. They took turns destroying it and building it back up again.

"yeah, i'm lining them up like a castle there's a king inside, and a naughty witch. Batman saves the king. can i have more glowsticks? a castle doesn't go like that, it goes like this"
Charlie

During the afternoon session he discussed what he had made in the morning with his friends and asked for help to build it again. They spent a lot of time in the afternoon creating a castle of light. **"it's all light now! our castle is done!"**

A few months later Charlie came into the Atelier and selected six torches. He stood them on end in a line around him on the edge of the table and discussed his new castle with his friend: **"this is my castle, it's like the other one but big!"**

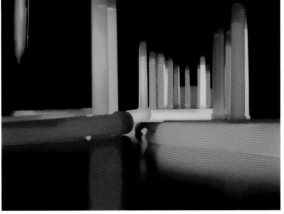

Zach was in the Atelier and glowsticks were available for the children to explore. Zach selected all of the blue glowsticks and held them up to his eyes, **"do you like my glasses?"** He then selected a couple of the green glowsticks and began to build an ellipse. He looked down at his pile of glowsticks and said: **"i need lots more blue, but there's none."** He chose a few more green ones and stood them in parallel lines along the table. He looked at his pile again, **"i need more ones. i guess i need these colours now"** pointing to some red glowsticks. He worked in this way through red, yellow, orange and pink.

ZACH'S GLOWSTICK CITY

"it's massive! a whole city! i made it! and towers!" Zach stood back and viewed his creation from a lower level and smiled.

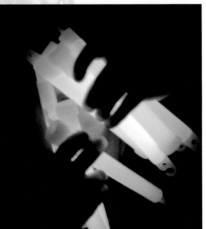

MAPPING LIGHT

As the project progressed, the children revisited a number of themes, one of the most significant was mapping light.

Children reworked their ideas about how to capture light's journey. An interesting experiment began when the pre-school section was involved in another project related to maps. They had been creating maps of the local area and of the forest they visit for forest school; and mapping their journeys to and from the library and the shops. At the same time they started mapping their torch lights on the page. Taking it in turns, the children would shine a torch light along a large piece of paper on the floor as their friends tracked the light with their pencils. This created a series of beautiful meandering lines wherever the light travelled. The children worked well in collaboration and developed their own systems for turn taking.

"can i be the light man?" Zachary asking his friends if he could shine the torch
"the light lines are gone!" Lachlan examining the drawing as they turned the lights off

"hahaha! you can't catch me!" Arden laughing, as he moved his torch quickly

Noting their sustained interest in torches, I introduced cardboard tubes and various open-ended resources for them to use with torchlight. The children used these to build vertically, on top of the torch light. They also used the overhead projector in this way and created interesting and dramatically lit tube towers of different sizes and shapes. Later, when I introduced coloured water in jars, this added a new element to their light construction; they could now work with colour that would vary depending on where their torch was positioned.

"a big light tower! with shadows!" **Harry**

MARK-MAKING AND COMPOSITIONS

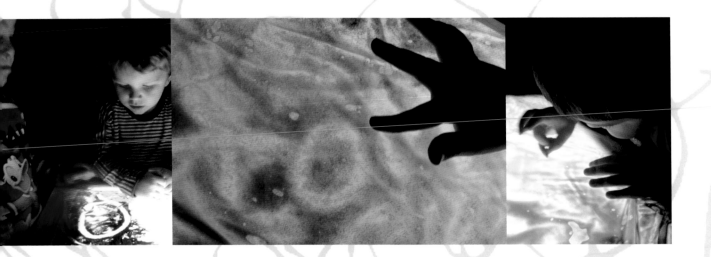

To offer more opportunities for mark-making, we used paint inside layers of plastic and worked with them on the light box. As they used their fingers to move the paint around between the layers, light would shine through. Thomas spent a long time using the lightbox, first using his finger to write a "T", then an "O" and an "M" before drawing a variety of shapes. Children experimented drawing with seashells, drinks lids, and other resources to create beautiful light and dark compositions.

"it's a different type of light" Gabrielle P.

"these ones glow! those don't, but these do. not those again. uh oh Zara, these don't either! no blue and green now. how about white ones? yes!"

Saffy experimenting with colour and black light

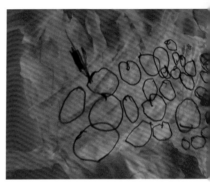

The children explored colour mixing at various stages of the project. They invented the perfect purple to represent our black light and experimented with layering glowsticks. They were keen to paint a picture which glowed. At this stage we had not provided any fluorescent paint. After some attempts with ordinary paint they realised they were not achieving the desired result. I introduced fluorescent paint to them which they used in natural light and in black light. They created fluorescent paintings on white backgrounds under the black light, the paper glowed; this led the children to experiment with white paint and black light, but the effects were not what they had imagined. Whilst the white paper glowed the white paint stayed dark.

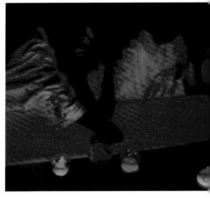

Stanley was in the Atelier exploring black light. There were a variety of resources available, some of which were light-reactive. Stanley first selected some green fabric and threw it in the air. He watched and smiled as it cascaded down. He then selected a bottle of glowing fluorescent paint and placed this in front of the mirrors which were attached to the black light: **"they glow on both mirrors!"** He moved closer to the mirrors and then away. **"can i have a draw of when the paint goes into the mirror?"** He chose some paper and a pencil and drew a rectangular shape with a circle at the top: **"this is the bottle. and i see some yellow. the yellow comes through onto the mirror on the other side. the paint's not there!"** When he finished this picture he drew it twice more, carefully observing the bottle each time.

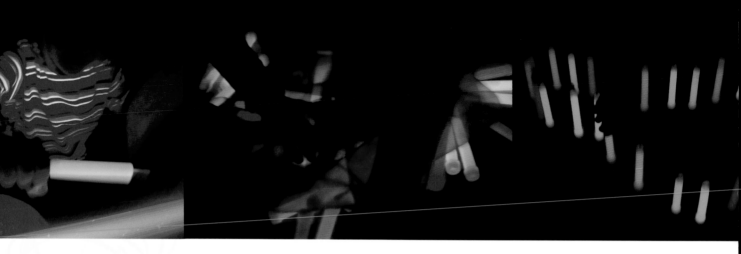

THE COLOUR OF LIGHT

"what's in there?"
Gabrielle P. holding up the glowstick and moving the liquid back and forth

"the glow's not working! maybe it's hiding!"
Keira

"when lights are normal, the light is bright and white" Lachlan

What does light look like...?

"it looks like fire! and a rocket! .. green sometimes!" Zach

"it looks like sparklers! or a moon. sometimes white, and sometimes yellow. and sometimes on shops different colours. it makes you hot... the SUN!" Madison

"it looks like blue" Olivia

"it's very bright. it has patterns on it" Emily

"stars" Gabrielle P.

"light is white!" Lachlan

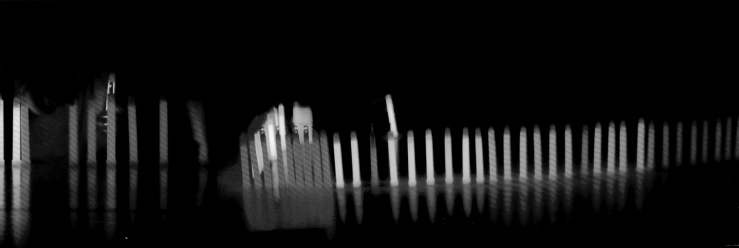

"glowsticks glow because they've got light in them. they come from halloween. glow is inside it" Zach

Colour was a recurrent theme throughout the project. The children were asked at various stages what they thought the colour of light was and their responses changed over time.

When working with glowsticks the children noted that light was not always white. They theorised about what was inside the glowsticks that made them glow, and recognised that after time they lost their 'glow'. The children combined the glowsticks with the black light and believed that this 'recharged' the glow.

"i made it glow again!"
Emilia shaking her glowstick

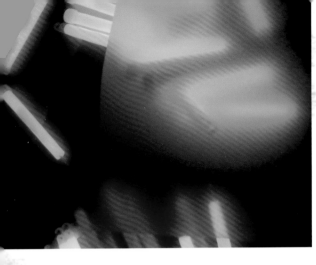

The children learnt about the diffusion of light by placing thick tracing paper over the glowsticks.

"if you put some paper over it, it changes" Keira

When black light was combined with the glowsticks the children noted the heightened intensity.

"it glows in the dark! it glows! it glows! it glows! when it's dark, it glows. there's light inside it. when we spin it, it glows. it glows when we do it fast and whennnnnnnn weeeeeee dooooooooo itttttttt slowwwwwwwwww it doesn't" Ela

They introduced colour-theory based games to their use of glowsticks which they created on their own. Lachlan spent an afternoon sharing with Evie how to play his game:

"there's a line of glowsticks on the light and we roll these ones. you have to do it really quick so it hits them. but sometimes they go wobbly" Lachlan

"let's shake them and then they will light! if we rub them with our hands then they will go into colours" Harry

Children noted that the glowsticks brightened when black light was added as did some of the colours on their clothes, their hair, and their teeth.

"my teeth were glowing 'cos of Angela's light"
Elliot

One event changed their perception of colour: Emily placed a brown plastic pot under the black light which turned fluorescent orange. When she was asked what colour it was she said **"orange of course"** and then when she turned the light on she saw it was brown and said **"where did the orange go?!"**

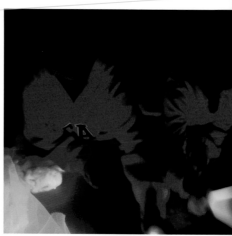

"the light glows blue things. when it's a different colour it doesn't glow like white"
Emily

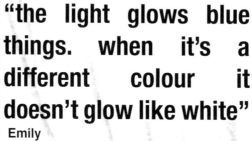

"we're glowing! we're glowing! we're glowing! We're gloooooooooooooowwwwwwii-iiiiiiiiinnnnnggg! we're glowing! we're glowing!"
Frankie and Charlie singing as they looked in the mirror, by the black light

"look, if we put them on the black light then the glow comes back" **Lachlan**

"you just can't see it properly because it glows in the dark! we need to turn the light off to see!" Emily

"black light. black mirrors. do you know yesterday i put my face in the mirror with Katie and we saw our teeth! they went different colours!"
Harry

Hi-visibility jackets, white t-shirts, cotton wool, fluorescent netting, and mirrors were available to the children and they spent time looking at the differences between black light's effect on white objects and on coloured objects. They identified that some colours would glow and others would not.

The children interacted with the black light in different ways, from quietly whispering about it to loudly singing together as they watched their fluorescent reflections in the mirrors.

"that one. this greeny glows the best. almost as good as white. we are glowing in here!"

Macey shouting to her friends as they entered the Atelier

Aidan was in the Atelier exploring the black light. He selected a piece of green fabric which glowed fluorescent. Mirrors were placed behind the black light so the children could see their reflections as they interacted with the resources.

"if you put the green fabric there you'll go green! i'm all green now! look at my big green face!"
Aidan looking in the mirror, as he moved the fabric closer to the light and the mirrors.

"it's glowing me! it's glowed all over my face! and my hands! i'm glowing!" **Leo looking in the mirror, moving the fluorescent green fabric around.**

"my top! it's glowing! my teeth are green. i'm glowing! look what i'm building. it's floating. i need to make this shape. look at this Angela, over here, it's dark and here it's glowing! it's doing a big glow. it's going to float up again. up up up into the sky. float! float! float! why does it glow here and not there?"

James, linking his glowsticks together and lifting them into the air

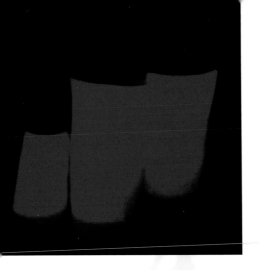

PAPER + LIGHT

Shredded paper was introduced with the black light and the children created a series of games.

Stanley was in the Atelier experimenting with black light and shredded paper. He approached the light and pointed to the edge where the paper was glowing. He ran his finger along the light and pointed to the end that was furthest from the light: **"those ones don't glow because they're far away from the light. only these ones glow."** Stanley spent a long time scrunching the shredded paper. He picked it up and carefully let it fall from his hands.

A 3D project, which included paper folding, had been ongoing for some time throughout the nursery. In the Atelier, the children were keen to experiment with their paper structures in conjunction with light sources. Elliot spent some time working with strips of paper on the light box. He placed his hand underneath the paper and above, commenting on the effects.

"i can see my hand! it made a shadow!" Elliot

"it's lighting underneath!" Elliot

INTERACTIVE LIGHTS

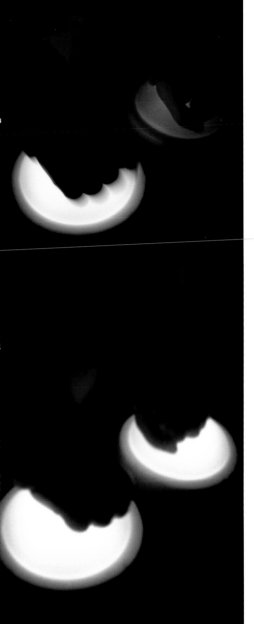

A range of interactive lights which responded to sound and touch, were provided for the children to explore.

Lachlan was in the Atelier investigating touch-sensitive lights. He pushed them to make the lights come on, moving his body from side to side and humming at the same time. Lachlan interacted physically with these lights, dancing and tapping out a rhythm on them like bongos. He then turned to the sound-activated lights and began singing to them: **"la la laaaaaa."**

When his friends came into the Atelier he was keen to share his experiences:

"everyone quiet and it will turn off, see?" Lachlan with sound activated light

"we need to switch lights on" Ashlei

"it makes noise! loud, loud noise!"
Ewa describing the sound of light

NOA SINGING TO LIGHT

Noa was in the Atelier exploring a sound-activated light. She sang to it in a low voice watching it as it lit up. She lowered her voice to barely a whisper and the light disappeared. **"where's it gone?"** As she spoke the light flickered on and off. **"it's there!"**, she exclaimed, and the light lit up again brightly. **"silly lights! where are they going?"** She began singing again to the lights, this time louder, and enjoyed watching them glow.

"i'm singing but maybe they want a present?" Noa selected a pencil and paper and drew an accurate picture of the light as a gift. Holding her picture up to the light she said, **"i drew you!"**

Noa smiled and continued to sing to the lights, noting the differences when she sang quietly or loudly and smiling between each variation.

"it's shining and flashing"
Stanley singing to his sound-activated light

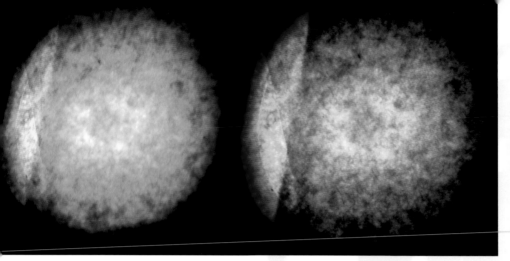

The children accessed coloured cellophane to cover their torches which changed the colour of the light. They used torches and tissue paper to create coloured light compositions on the ceiling of the Atelier.

LAYERING COLOUR WITH LIGHT

Jasper was in the Atelier experimenting with transparency and opacity. He layered different colours of cellophane and wrapped them around the torch, shining it onto the ceiling. He removed the layers one by one, noting how his composition on the ceiling changed each time. He included a piece of brown packing paper in his investigations, placing it onto the large torch and traced the edges of the torch shining through the paper in a series of spiral movements. Jasper spent about 30 minutes exploring this and continued his investigations in the afternoon.

"the colours are red" **Jasper**

"i'm wrapping colours around it so it changes.
"i can see a little bit! but if i move that it changes
the colour"
Noa wrapping coloured cellophane around the end of her torch.

Aidan was in the Atelier investigating transparency and opacity using a variety of cellophane, fabrics and papers with large and small torches. He spent some time placing tissue paper and cellophane in different colours on top of the torches. **"it's a rainbow! i made a rainbow on the ceiling. red! red! that's the colour on here and now it's up there! i think that's gonna be a different colour with green. who wants to see how to do a rainbow? it was making a rainbow. now it's making dark green."** Aidan sang a song as he selected only the green cellophane: **"just one colour on for now. just one colour, just one colour, just! one! colour!"**

"the light is white. it's changed now, the light is not so bright but it's a different colour now. i can still see it"
Caitlin adding yellow cellophane onto her torch

"my one's turning different blue!"

Charlie adding light blue cellophane on top of a blue glowstick

"i put it red on blue. now it's purple" **Juliusz**

Layering and colour mixing often occurred spontaneously; whether it was cellophane being laid over glowsticks, glowsticks themselves being layered, or using the overhead projector to create different colours with multiple layers of cellophane.

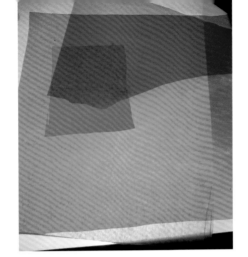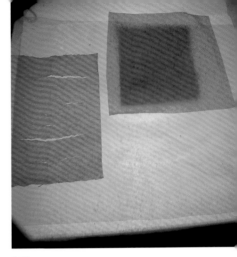

"Angela! there's a rainbow in there!"

Aidan pointing into the base of the overhead projector, where he could see a spectrum of light reflected from the mirror above

We introduced a small flip book to the children - when you flipped the pages, a rainbow would appear. The children took turns trying to "catch a rainbow" in their hands. A group of children worked together to create a rainbow lining up coloured felt tip pens. When they had all the available colours, they scoured the Atelier for other coloured items to add to their rainbow collage.

"you turn it and move the pages and it grows a rainbow out of it!"

Olivia explaining how to use the rainbow flip book

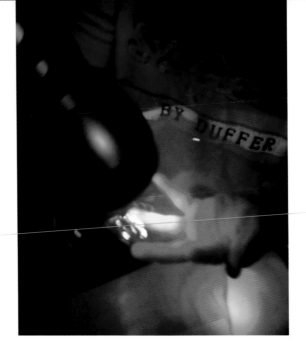

TRANSPARENCY VS. OPACITY

Children continued to experiment with colour and with transparency versus opacity. A variety of papers were available for the children to combine with their torches.

LACHLAN + ASHLEI
"ok, now how many layers?" Lachlan asked Ashlei, as he placed two layers of green cellophane onto a torch. **"there's two greens. now wait! don't look! don't look!"**

Ashlei added a layer of brown paper onto the torch and said: **"there's too many! i can't see the light!"**

Lachlan: **"it's because there's one that isn't see through. you can't see through this one because it's big and brown"**

Ashlei: **"why can't i see through it?"** lifting up the brown paper.

Lachlan: **"it's too big. it's what Angela said you can't see through. it's *oplate*"**

ELLIOT

Elliot was in the Atelier exploring transparency and opacity, and trying to see how far light would travel through layers of paper. He put a single layer of red cellophane on top of the torch: **"it can travel! it went all the way through to the ceiling!"** Elliot continued to explore different layer combinations, culminating with brown packing paper and exclaims: **"it's stopped travelling!"** He then removed all the layers and began again with red, carefully noting the result each time he added a new layer. When he got to the brown paper he held it up to the light to test its transparency and put it back down on the table unused.

INSIDE LIGHT MEETS OUTSIDE LIGHT

In discussion, Lewis, Emily, Lily, Harry and Elliot, had decided on an interesting proposition - to make the natural light outside meet the artificial light inside.

The Atelier was blacked out and they hung glowsticks on the pull-string for the blackout blind, adding more and more until the weight of the glowsticks finally made the blind shoot up and the sunshine come streaming in.

"they're on the door because i want it to be light and everyone know where they're going. also maybe that light outside can find our lights in here!" **Emily**

"the light found us!"
Emily

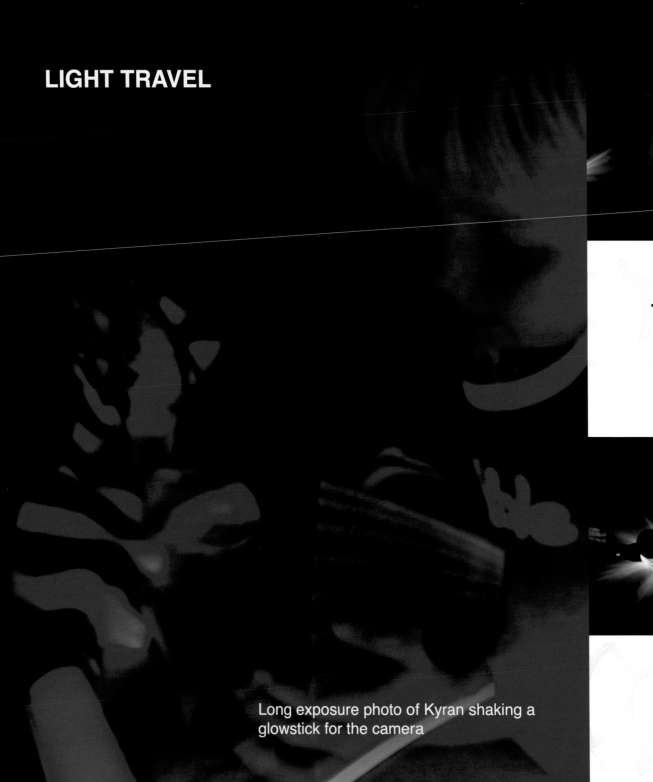

LIGHT TRAVEL

Long exposure photo of Kyran shaking a glowstick for the camera

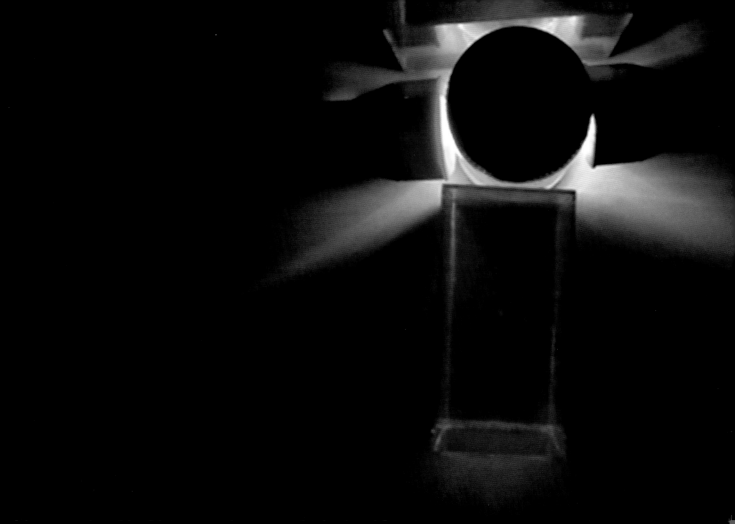

To extend the children's experiments about how light travels, I introduced pots of water, some with colour added, others with metallic tinsel or glass marbles. Children lined the jars up and counted how many pots their torchlight would shine through before it faded to nothing. Madison was absorbed by the torchlight interacting with tinsel in the water. She turned the pot clockwise and counter-clockwise, observing the different directions the tinsel would travel in. Children also experimented with the effect that the size of the torch had on the distance the light could travel. They shone torchlight through different coloured waters onto each other.

HARRY

Harry was in the Atelier experimenting with torches and water. He had been involved in some discussion about how far light could travel through water. **"it's gone red because i'm shining it in there and that's called red light. when i put the light through it first and don't do that, it doesn't shine. when i put it close and shine it goes red and it puts red on the bottles. if i put my hand behind here it makes yellow. it's red when i do that!"** Harry saw his hand glowing red from the light even though it was behind the yellow water: **"if you shine this into the light, you don't see it. there's still a candle in there though."**

Harry used two torches, one which gave off a blue light and another a yellow light and shone one into the other: **"if i turn it off you can see purple in it, if i turn it on, you can't."**

Harry shone the blue torch through the red water: **"red and blue make purple!"**

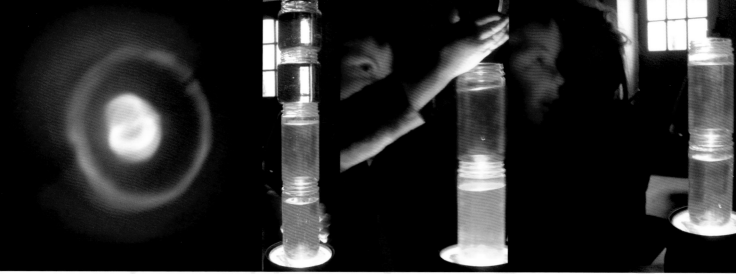

ELLIOT

Harry was shining a torch through red water, making his friends glow red. "**how did you do that?**" asked Elliot. "**i can see red but inside between those ones. what if we go through this way?**" Elliot shone the torch on the other side of the jar towards me: "**it's red and red i made Angela red! it's turning orange and red!**"

Elliot continued to experiment changing the order of the coloured jars he was stacking on top of the torchlight; and asking questions as he investigated. He made an interesting discovery by shining another torch at the point where the two colours meet: "**how's that then? if you do that** (shine the torch) **and go in there** (shine it between the red and yellow water jars) **it mixes them. when i do that my hand goes orange. when i pick it up and go there it glows. what happens if i shine it this way? if we put that jar there what happens? it's still red. now, between those ones and between those ones, they go there and they're still red! this one, the heaviest one of all, still goes red.**"

During this experiment Elliot noted that the jars with lids on stopped the light travelling through. "**you put the wrong one on. put this one on. the red's gone in there. if we put this one on top, it's gone. that one's a jar. you have to stop putting the lid on! she has to take the lid off!!!**"

ARDEN

Arden was in the Atelier experimenting with light and water. He shone a torch into the water tray; a friend came in and asked him what was happening, **"we're trying to see when the light goes through."** Arden moved over to the table where there were a number of water jars containing coloured water and shone his torch through a line of the jars, turning it on and off. **"if i turn it off, we can't see the colours but if i turn it on, we can see them shining."** He moved the torch along the line of jars, noting the changes: **"water's white when lights are white"**

"if Arden shines it there i can see the light shining all the way through. it's getting bigger and changing different colours! it's mixing the colours in the water line. we have 5 waters in our water line and the light works"
Noa

"1, 2, 3, 4, 5 ...
i want to try it with the little one"
Mya using a smaller torch

"i'm pointing it at the window. it makes it orange on that side and on that side too"
Axel

"the water's going red! how cool is that Angela?!" Aidan

"it's made it all red. it's all yellowy. now i'm going to make these both red" Natalie

"if you shine it there it makes red go in my eyes"
Zach talking to Axel who was shining a torch through red water

"what about if we do it on a sparkly one? what about if we do this one? no light on these ones, then i will move it so it shines"
Lachlan, trying moving a jar of water around so he could see the tinsel sparkle

REFLECTING LIGHT

In the Atelier small mirrors hung from the ceiling, and mirrored boards and mirrored lettering were accessible to the children.

"if i shine it there it makes a number seven!" Charlie

CHARLIE

Charlie was in the Atelier one morning, exploring different types of paper with a torch. He shone his torch around the room and smiled as he noticed a reflection. His torchlight caught some mirrored letters and the 'L' reflected onto the wall. Charlie exclaimed to his friend: **"if i shine it there it makes a number seven!"** His friend shone his torch in the same place, too. There was much discussion about how mirrors reflect light.

Later that day, Charlie shone a torch on the mirrored letters again, exclaiming: **"it's reflecting!"**

Charlie continued to investigate reflections with the torch and showed his friends how to achieve the same effect.

"there's light coming through..."

"it's coming from under"

STANLEY

Stanley was investigating mirrored paper with a magnifying glass: **"there's light coming through?"** he asked me. I asked him where he thought the light was coming from. **"it's coming from under!"**

Stanley selected a different magnifying glass to see if the light persisted: **"does it go with this one?"** Stanley tested out different magnifying glasses, turning the paper over and over trying to find the source of the light. After some time he looked up to the ceiling and smiled looking back down at the mirror. He pointed to the mirrored paper, demonstrating that he had discovered the source of the light to be the spotlight on the ceiling of the Atelier.

Kyran measuring distance moving a torch up and down

The children created games trying to catch light from each other's torches, chasing the beams around the room. They discussed distances: would it be brighter if we moved closer? How can we reach it? Can we stretch? **"maybe if I go closer it'll be brighter"** This led to a discussion about whether light might travel around corners:

"i saw the sun, i saw the sun. it followed us, i saw the sun come out then it went away when we went round the corner" Lachlan

JAMES
James shone a torch around the room and onto a green chair. **"my light is green!"** he shouted. I asked him what happened to the light when it shone onto the table. James diverted his beam to shine on the Atelier table: **"it's white! where did the green go?"** James shone his torch back to the green chair. **"the chair is green! ohhhh!"** James spent much of the day using the torch and shining it onto different coloured objects.

TRANSPARENCY

"transparent – like trans and parents" **Noa**

"this is transparent because it comes out. Angela, when you can see through it, it's transparent" **Elliot**

"i can see through this one" **Madison**

"transparent means you CAN see through it, and opaque means you can't" **Lachlan**

Iggy and Elliot were interacting with Mylar strips (translucent paper) hanging from the ceiling in the Atelier above the light box. They selected a number of random objects from the room and held them in front of the Mylar:

Iggy: *"what can glow?"*
Elliot: *"does this glow?"*
Iggy: *"i think this is gonna glow"*
Elliot: *"let's see. oh wow! do you see it glowing?"*
Iggy: *"this one REALLY glows!"*
Elliot: *"probably the best glow, it is"*
Iggy: *"but what about this one?"*
Elliot: *"hold it there"*
Iggy: *"no, it needs to go here for it to be best"*
Elliot: *"i'll put it there to glow very strong"*

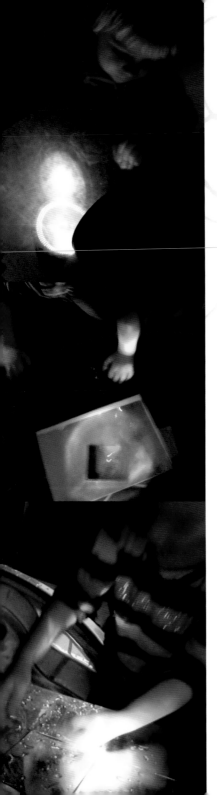

REVISITING LIGHT TRAVEL

Following on from their earlier experiments shining torchlight through jars of coloured water, the children were keen to investigate further. They split light into different spectrums using water, mirrors, prisms and torches. They revisited and extended their earlier experiments with cellophane and torches, this time choosing to combine these with reflective surfaces to see how it affected the light. They also continued their experiments with light and paper, introducing a wider selection of papers.

"it goes into it and light comes out in a line. now orange is coming out. it's wobbling the sparkles. i'm making it on the wall! it's on the wall! now the orange is on the wall, behind the boxes. it went around."

Keira, shaking the pots of water around and shining her torch through them

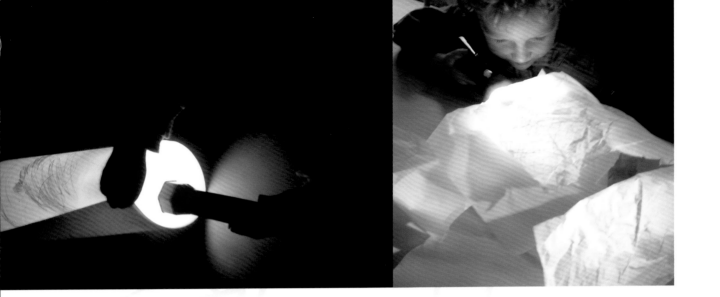

"i'm wrapping colours around it so it changes...we're trying to see how light travels" Noa

Hughie was experimenting with mirrors and light and selected a small torch. He moved the torchlight around the table, watching it dart back and forth. He shone it onto the ceiling: **"oh no! it's gone! look! up there,"** pointing to the ceiling. He continued to direct the beam around the room, each time exclaiming: **"there's the light! there's the light!"**

His beam caught a mirror and it lit up his face. He squinted and exclaimed, **"it's Hughie! it's there!"**

"look what's happening! it's going red to that glass!"

Emily shone her torch through a jar of red water and into a jar of clear water and noted the result

"look! it's going red through the water and on that side!" Harry

"when loads of light gets inside it goes bright"

Emily holding a torchlight up to a water-filled prism

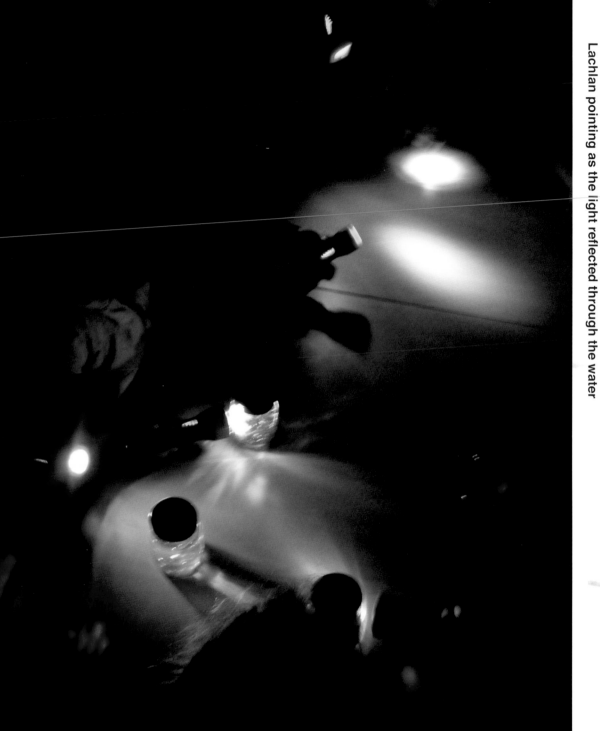

"i see light there"

Lachlan pointing as the light reflected through the water

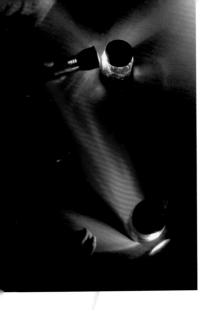
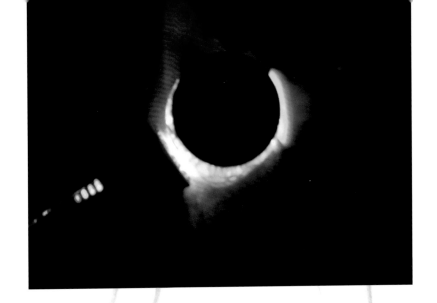

"it's going red then wobbling about. when i turn it off it doesn't shine because the torch is off. then when it's on the torch is shining through it and going out. if you turn it to one side it still glows. if you turn it forwards it goes more red. the torch lights it out, like electricity! electricity inside the torch. the light comes out of the torch. it goes straight across and along there. i need a red felt tip." Stanley

Stanley selected a red felt tip pen and some paper to draw the results of his experiment.

"when you turn the light off it goes to sleep" James

"Angela, it looks a bit like Star Wars" Aidan

"my hand's gone yellow because i'm shining it through the yellow"
Gabrielle P.

"look! it's making the water glow up" Emily

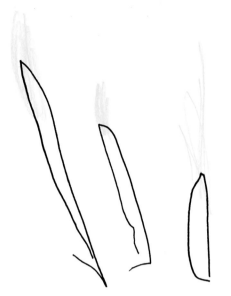

CANDLELIGHT

Some of the children had been making fires during their Forest School sessions and discussed how light looked like fire. I chose to introduce candlelight as a natural light source and the pre-school section spent a day living just by candlelight. The children chose to draw candlelight, and many of them were fascinated by the fact that it was on fire.

Arden had an interesting theory: when one of the candles with a short wick wouldn't light, he suggested that this specific candle might be 'allergic' to fire.

The children became quite enamoured with the candlelight and wanted to keep the candles safe, perhaps like the candlelight made them feel. They decided to create clay candle holders to look after their candles.

"it's going bigger and bigger. it's stronger! it's gonna hide! it's hiding.." Kyran

CONCLUSION

"Creativity seems to emerge from multiple experiences, coupled with a well-supported development of personal resources, including a sense of freedom to venture beyond the known."

Loris Malaguzzi

Although this project spanned a seven month period, I often felt the children's questions and discussions merited more time to do them justice. The project involved a number of provocations and solicited many theories and hypotheses from the children. We had the opportunity to investigate some of these but others will have been left unexplored. It is our experience that unexplored theories often resurface in future project work.

Whether working in groups, in pairs or alone, children brought their creative thinking to every aspect of this theme. I believe they developed a strong understanding of many properties of light; scaffolding their own learning and at the same time, learning how to learn. I loved the connections they made and the intimacy they created with light as well as the enthusiasm they brought to each session.

I believe that the resources, the environment and a culture of listening to children, taking their theories seriously, contributed to the scope of their learning. I often found many of their questions challenging and enjoyed learning alongside the children and found inspiration for my own work from their ideas.

Following this project the children continued to make comments which underscored their learning, and they maintained a deep interest in light and shadow. I believe that the children have developed a heightened sensibility to a universal and enduring theme - as one of the children profoundly commented, **"light is everywhere."**